Crisis Management

HOW TO MANAGE PERSONAL LIFE CRISES

Keeler Bryson

Vision Writers Publishing, LLC

Sherwood, AR

Keeler Bryson/Vision Writers Publishing, LLC
P.O. Box 6516
Sherwood, AR 72124
www.KeelerBryson.com

©2013 BookDesignTemplates.com

Crisis Management: How To Manage Personal Life Crises
Keeler Bryson. —1st ed.
ISBN 978-0615939803

Contents

Acknowledgements

To Almighty God, Thank You for gifting me with the skill, ability and focus to write this book. I Thank You for all the past crises in my life, for I now realize that they were preparing me with life experiences and valuable lessons, in order to share them with others, so that they may live a more empowering life. Thank You for Instinct and Revelation.

To my loving, supportive and hardworking husband, Grover, Thank you for your commitment and dedication to "Team Bryson," through the good and bad times. Thank you for never wavering in your love for me and our daughters. I know how much God loves me by the amazing husband you are to me.

To my daughters, Whitney and Miracle, you girls make me proud.

To my mom, Thank you for raising me to be who I am today. Thank you for all the sacrifices you made to make sure I had what I needed.

To Millicent Ross, Thank you for always blessing me with journals. Each time you bought me one, it was a reminder from God to write my book.

To Evangelist Jeanette Ester, that day at church, in the church library, when you prophesied to me that I would write a book, I could not fathom how it would come together and happen. Thank you for allowing God to speak through you.

Dedication To Reader

Dear reader:

God had you on His mind when He unctioned me to write this book. Embrace this book and its principles; for in applying them you will experience the miraculous power of God in your life crises. Fear not, only believe.

Releasing your potential is simply becoming yourself as God our Creator originally intended.

—George Fraser

Introduction

There's so much going on in the world today. People are troubled in some way or another; problems, obstacles, setbacks, disappointment, loss- -crisis. I don't know about you, but I've had a good portion of crisis in my life. Some were voluntary, the rest involuntary. I'm okay with going through my share of crises; however, it can be extremely overwhelming when the crisis multiplies and intensifies. When we look at the world today, it seem like crises are on the rise, everywhere you look, like never before. I've come to realize that one thing we can count on is a life crisis.

With that in mind, it would behoove us to educate, equip and coach ourselves on how to make it through a variety of crises. For without the proper preparation, we subject ourselves to the possibility of becoming dependent on anti-depressants, street drugs, alcohol, weight loss/gain, health problems, suicide and/or homicide. Without proper crisis preparation/teaching, we'll become over-whelmed and will eventually SNAP!

It's interesting how just recently in the news, there have been stories of men, women and children who went to work or school and snapped. They went to Capitol Hill and snapped. They went to church and snapped. Each time I see these types of events on the news, my heart is touched because it could have been me. I often think, "If only these folks had someone or way to get coaching/training to help guide them through the difficult moments of their crisis." With the right coaching and skills, we can overcome casualties of a crisis: addiction to prescription drugs, street drug use, alcoholism, weight loss/gain, health problems brought on by stress, temporary mental meltdowns/breakdowns, thoughts of suicide and homicide, depression and oppression, hair loss, sudden outbursts of crying, accelerated aging, excessive sleeping, irritability, etc.

We all remember the secretary at the elementary school in Decatur, GA who talked down the gunman with an

AK-47 who had come to the school to murder as many people as he possibly could. Somehow the secretary found the courage to reach out to the gunman by sharing her story of pain and disappointment, thereby convincing the gunman that he shouldn't go through with killing anyone. She told the gunman we all are going through some sort of problem, but we have to keep believing things will get better for us. She basically was telling him don't do something you'll regret later because what looks bad right now can only get worse, if we do the wrong thing. All we need is another day. Besides, no storm lasts forever.

With this in mind, I'm writing this book for those who are in crisis as a tool or resource to coach you through your crisis. I've been through many crises and feel God would have me use my experiences to teach and encourage others through theirs. You might be like me, a private person. And as a result of this, whenever I'm in a crisis, I usually don't share what I'm going through with people. This is what you call a "silent sufferer." In being a silent suffer, it allowed me to be coached by God in a unique way which resulted in the lessons I'm about to discuss in this book. Sometimes sharing your crisis with others who are not experienced and qualified to help, is not always wise to do. In fact, sharing your crisis with others can sometimes make things worse, if you share it with the wrong person. I also admit that withholding, from someone who's proven they can be trusted, is sometimes not good either. In either case, this book will be beneficial to you. In this book I will discuss what a crisis is, the role of a coach in a crisis, the types of crises you're likely to encounter and the twelve steps of making it successfully through a crisis. It is my intent, via this book, for each reader to become their own crisis coach.

It's possible some might have issue with this book advocating coaching yourself through a crisis, as many believe in getting outside professional help. I get that. My response to that is, in Scripture, there are many examples of people who were in crisis and they made it through their crisis without "outside help." They did it with "Inside Help." What is "Inside Help?" It's help that comes from God Himself. It's coaching that comes from the God of the Universe. This is coaching that comes from the "The Source." Besides, who knows better than God how we're to come through a crisis? In fact, in many cases, many people are not coming successfully through their crisis because they've received ineffective coaching from everyone except, "The Source"- - God. His coaching is one-on-one, efficient, effective and edifying/elevating. I believe one of the byproducts of experiencing a crisis is that it develops us into quality and effective overcomers so that we in turn are qualified to coach/help others through the crises we've already been through. Moreover, how can we effectively coach others if we first don't know how to help ourselves? Einstein once said, "All true learning is experience. Everything else is just information." Sometimes the only way we can discover our God-given true power is by living through a crisis.

CHAPTER 1

What is a Crisis?

F irst off, let's define what a crisis is and what a coach is. I don't mean to insult your intelligence, but for clarity sake and deeper understanding, I'd like to take a look into the meaning of these two words.

Crisis Defined:

Just looking at the word, I see the root word cri or cry, which definitely signals crying. Because when you're in an intense crisis, it will at some point make you cry! According to online Etymology Dictionary, crisis means:

- turning point in a disease;
- judgment, result of a trial;

2 • KEELER BRYSON

- selection;
- to sift;
- separate;

According to Dictionary.com, crisis is:

- a stage in a sequence of events at which the trend of all future events, especially for better or worse is determined
- a condition of instability or danger, as in social, economic, political or international affairs leading to decisive change
- dramatic emotional or circumstantial upheaval in a person's life
- sudden change

If you've ever been in a crisis, then you agree that these definitions accurately describe a crisis. It is a turning point of dis-ease and you do feel like you're in judgment or some sort of trial. You feel selected, as if you're the only one going through the crisis. You feel picked on. You're asking, "Why me?"

Another definition is, to sift. In Scripture, Jesus told Peter Satan desired to have him so he could sift him like wheat. This is not like the sifting we normally do with flour. The sifting Satan desired to do was a violent separating and tearing apart. Satan desired to separate Peter from God's goodness and God's way. He wanted to snatch God's word out of Peter's heart and mind. Satan wants to pull on the seams that join our marriages, families, relationships and lives together. He wants to wear thin the fabric of our faith. Crisis is a time of intense feelings of instability, danger, dramatic emotional or circumstantial upheaval, sudden change, for worse.

But through this book, we are given the opportunity to prepare and strengthen ourselves for future crises. For according to Scripture, more perilous days are ahead. But through this book, you will be taught how to be pre-

pared, recover and grow from the setbacks of a crisis.

CHAPTER 2

What is the Role of a Coach?

Coach Defined:

According to Dictionary.com, a coach is:

- a person who trains an athlete or team of athletes to give instruction or advice
- to instruct
- to tutor, as one who carries the student through examinations

A coach is one who seize upon defeat and victory as "teachable moments" - - opportunities to build an athlete's self- confidence, positive character traits, such as determination, courage, empathy and commitment. A coach carries/tutors the student through examinations.

A coach develops internal motivation training and development to achieve a goal. This is what I believe God is working on developing within each of us through this book since most of us are in the process of developing "the coach" within us. He wants us to learn, through Him, how to be our own crises coach. With so many people suffering these days, it can sometimes be difficult to find someone with an encouraging word because they're going through their own crisis too.

This crisis thing has become so bad until we're now seeing Pastor's committing suicide, as a result of the pressures of life. This is a warning to us to learn how to coach and encourage ourselves, so that in case no one's around to coach us, we're well able to do it ourselves, as well as for others. I believe part of the reason Pastors are committing suicide, is because they've become "hostages of pride and/or embarrassment." Both will lock you deeper into your crisis because you're too arrogant to admit you need help or too embarrassed about the type of crisis you're in. When in a crisis, do not allow pride or embarrassment to hold you hostage, as it's nearly impossible to get help when you do this.

A coach is an encourager. Scripture talks about how at one point in David's life, he was in a major crisis and felt alone to the point that he had to encourage himself. In other words, he had to coach his self into a state of encouragement. He had to become his own trainer, tutor and instructor, which yielded the self-confidence, courage and determination to go on and not quit. He made up his mind to be committed, no matter how bad his crisis was. When we're in crisis, from the very beginning of it, we've got to decide that in spite of the sudden, dramatic changes of instability, danger and emotional upheaval, we're going to ride the crisis out, seize the teachable moments and ultimately possess the trophy of triumph! If we have this perspective, we'll embrace the crisis better, rather than resisting it, complaining and over reacting.

There are several books written about managing business/corporate crises, but very few written on how to manage our individual life crises. Just like businesses and corporations have crisis management plans and directives, so should we as individuals. We need to know how to manage our own personal life crises. This book serves to meet this need. After all, crisis is a part of life.

We must accept the fact that at some point in life, we're going to have a major crisis. We must also realize: 1) that crisis is just like the definition - - a stage in a sequence of events. This means it will not be over until the sequence of events have taken place; 2) you're about to enter a turning point. This turning point will be for the better, not the worse, even though it doesn't seem like it at first; 3) the crisis is a time of judgment to demonstrate ability, capacity, wisdom/intelligence, discernment and balanced view points.

Think about it, every soldier and athlete endure an intense level of training and preparation for their respective vocations. They are already aware of what is required and expected of them. In other words, they don't enter in or join in misinformed. They anticipate working hard, suffering physically, long hours of training and practice, stress, body aches and pain, media attacks, hate from critics, etc. Yet they stay the course. They learn how to master the steps of performing well under pressure. They remain focused, knowing their efforts will lead them to their goal.

CHAPTER 3

Types of Crises

Crises can either be self-inflicted, God-inflicted or a combination of both. Self-inflicted crises are crises we create due to the choices and/or decisions (good or bad) we've made. A God-inflicted crisis is a crisis that arises because God has chosen to use us for His glory. This type of crisis comes so that God can prepare, ordain, mature and/or bless us. At first, however, it doesn't feel or appear that it's meant to bless us. In **Scripture Job said,** "Though he slay me, yet will I trust in him:" Though it may seem like God is slaying us, we must trust Him.

From Scripture, I've identified nine potential crises we're most likely to encounter in life at some point.

- Character Crisis
- Property Crisis
- Children Crisis
- Health Crisis
- Relationship Crisis
- Financial Crisis
- Reputation Crisis
- Destiny/Purpose Crisis
- Death Crisis

It's been said that, "Bad things happen to good people." Many would agree that only bad people should have to experience a crisis. But the truth is, no matter how good of a person we try to be, we're not exempt from crisis. Scripture says Job was blameless, upright, one who feared God and shunned evil. How could someone with character like this be subject to one hard-hitting crisis after another? Had Job been a wicked person, we'd understand why he was going through such a difficult time. Job is an eternal reminder that bad things do happen to good people. In fact, crises will sometimes come into our lives simply because we're blameless, upright, fear God and shun evil. Conversely, sometimes crises can also come into our lives because of fear, our unbelief or the words we've spoken. Job said, "The thing I've feared most has come upon me." This lets us know that our fears and unbelief can become our reality. So we must be careful how we think, as well as what we speak.

God had so much confidence in Job to the point He bragged on him to Satan. God used the crisis in Job's life to show the world his steadfast integrity, tenacity, loyalty and love for Him even in the midst of his hard-hitting, knock down crisis. With this in mind, we must consider going through our crisis an honor and privilege, not a curse. God only calls the best of the best. This means if He has chosen you, then it's a sign you possess the grace and ability to come out with the victory. Crisis can come into our lives in nine ways. They can come one at a time, in multiples or all at once. Job went through all nine. If you're only dealing with a crisis in one area right now, stop and give God thanks for that! The stronger you are spiritually the more likely you are to experience multiple crises. Whether you're going through one crisis or all nine at the same time, just know the ability to come out with the victory is within you. Make up your mind to go through!

Character Crisis

In Scripture, it says Job was blameless, upright, feared God and shunned evil. The devil and his kingdom despise this kind of person and is always out to prove that this person, this "Mr. or Ms. Goodie-too-shoe" is not the good person they appear to be. After all, nobody's perfect, right? Have you ever noticed how, for example at work, there could be an employee who's always at work, on time, their work is superb, they have a can do attitude, never complain, etc. The employees who are slackers, late, complaining all the time will begin to pick on and talk about the good worker, and ultimately try to turn the good employee into a poor worker, as they are or they try to make them feel bad because they have a strong work ethic. The slackers are sorry workers and want everyone else to be a sorry worker with them, because the good workers expose the bad worker's poor work ethic. This is exactly what Satan did to Job and he continues to do to us. He attempts to attack our character because we make him look bad. In spite of all Job had gone through, he ended up proving to be the man God said he was and proved the devil was a liar about who he was. This lets us know that the devil does not know what he's talking about. He does not know "all things," only God does. So why should we even listen to him?

Property Crisis

Scripture talks about how Job's eldest son's house was destroyed by a great wind. Speaking from experience, the loss of your property/home can be extremely devastating. All that you've worked hard for is gone without a reason, warning or apology. To be homeless, whether as a result of some sort of natural storm, act of God, divorce or foreclosure, etc., it can be one of the hardest moments you will ever go through. You will have a feeling of wandering. You will feel lost and con- fused. I remember these feelings all too well from even- tually losing our dream home to foreclosure.

What's interesting about the whole situation is that prior to the foreclosure, I kept having a re-occurring dream of a whitish tornado coming towards my dream home. Each time I had this dream, I was always able to pray the tor- nado away from hitting my house. But the last dream I had, I was unable to pray it away. This time the tornado partially damaged our house. I knew then that trouble was coming to my house. What's even more interesting is that after we foreclosed on the house, I haven't had the re-occurring dream. God was warning me all along that trouble was coming.

After God had previously delivered us from foreclosing on our dream home, via the loan modification, things were going well for a while and then I finally became pregnant and successfully delivered our second child. At the time, I was asking God, "Why the baby now?" Now look at how I'm acting. After all I'd been through with miscarriages and now my promise was at the threshold of my door and instead of immediately rejoicing, I'm cross examining God about His timing. I remember wondering why would God wait until we get into our dream house, where we are already running a tight budget and then decide now is the time for us to have our miracle child. What a sense of timing God has! I was extremely concerned with how we would be able to afford the added expenses that come with having a baby (i.e. doctor bills, diapers, clothes, daycare, baby food, etc.). As you can imagine, I had mixed feelings. On one hand, it was the best of times and on the other, it felt like the worst of times. Nonetheless, here we go again with the foreclosure drama. After the baby was born, my husband goes and gets a part-time job to try to cover some of the new expenses, but it was not enough. This time the bank wouldn't modify our loan. This time the foreclosure was going down.

Looking back, it needed to happen because we just couldn't afford it with the new baby and all. We lost our dream home. We ended up filing bankruptcy again, in order to resolve the deficiency on our mortgage loan. This was a double hit. We ended up moving into a 1200 square foot rent house. It was small! We had to put half of our belongings in storage. I remember asking God why? I couldn't believe it. It was like a bad dream. I was lost inside because I never thought, in a zillion years, I would have to go through this. I felt that I didn't deserve this. I didn't know whether we'd recover from this or whether we'd be able get another house one day. I remember wondering what people would think. I remember feeling so emotionally numb. This shook the very foundation of me, my belief system, my faith, my positive outlook on life, my resilience and my hope. Little did I know, but the loss of our home would cause us to enter a Paradigm Shift.

A Paradigm Shift is very powerful! A Paradigm Shift is an announcement that you're stuck, out of balance and that the real you and your real life wants to come forth. Back then I wasn't happy about this at all, but I'm so very grateful for it now. It changed me in ways and areas that I didn't even know needed to be changed. At any rate, we had to deal with the stress of finding somewhere else to live. We went out one Sunday morning looking for rental property. On our first attempt, we found a prospect. My husband wanted to pursue it, but I didn't. I wanted something newer. I was trying to find a rental property that didn't give the appearance that we were going through financial problems. In looking back, this behavior proved the need for the Paradigm Shift that was beginning to take place in my life at that time, as I had not been living authentically. I had given too much of myself away to the church I belonged to at the time, to belief systems I didn't agree with and to the drama of family members. I had created an image and lifestyle of "going along, to get along." I was doing what these individuals wanted, at the expense of giving up what I wanted. As a result, I was not living life as the real and true Keeler. But now I do! I'm free within and no longer torn between conflicting opinions and beliefs. I now live authentically and no longer by what others think I should do. This is real freedom and deliverance! So many people can't say this, as they're living a life they believe pleases others or a life others said they should live or a life that demands they "go along in order to get along." The loss of our home...The Paradigm Shift, birthed The Real Keeler. I found myself! I'm grateful for it too. Now God can truly and uninhibitedly use me because I'm no longer controlled by the beliefs, opinions and systems of others.

I'm no longer living under a false, dumbing down, people pleasing persona, which is bondage!

At any rate, we continued to look for something newer, but found nothing because our credit at the time made it difficult to find other options. So we ended up renting the first one we saw. Little did we know, but it was our divine connection. This house would be God's temporary holding space for us. It would be a place where there would be a renewing of our minds, a place of learning new life lessons, a place for God to prepare us for our next chapter and it was a place of no more revolving, but evolving, a place of transformation. Although I hated where we were, God would use it for His glory and give us a story. And even though I resented the place we were in, I trusted God enough, from experience, to know there was a greater purpose for what we were dealing with. We were temporarily in a small place, but God was doing BIG things there. Sometimes God will allow us to lose what we treasure most in order to get our attention on what He wants the most. I lost my home, but I birthed my second child. I lost my home, but I found myself. We lost our home, but in the end, God gave us another one. He is the restorer of our souls, as well as the property we've lost!

Children Crisis

Scriptures talks about how Job experienced a crisis with his children as a result of their death. In this section, my focus is on parents/guardians who encounter crisis with their children due to peer pressure, bullying, incarceration, drugs and alcohol, sexual issues, dating/relationship issues, etc. Children today face way more temptations than I faced when I was young, as a result of increased moral decay in this country. I was brought up with good morals and I in turn use those same teachings with my daughters. Unfortunately, many parents are not raising their children in this same way and as a result, their children become negative influencers to children who were raised like I was. And there's an abundance of children out there who are lost, parentless, troubled, rebellious, bitter and who have little to no morals. Regrettably, they appear to be the "cool kid" with "cool parents" to their peers. This creates peer pressure to become like them, which in turn creates upheaval and crisis in the parent/child relationship of children who were raised the opposite of the so called "cool kids." Young people believe their identity is their likeability. So they try to do whatever it takes in order to be liked by the so called cool/popular kids, in an effort to get an identity of being cool or popular as well.

Conversely, every day many parents are fighting to protect their children from being sucked into the status quo of loose and perverted morals and degrading choices and decisions that are often done in an attempt to fit in with those who are misfits. When you turn on the television, all day long it reflects nudity, casual bed/sex partners, sexual innuendos, foul language and contemptible expressions of art. We see disrespect and dishonor towards the president, all the way down to every other form of leadership in this country. Every day parents are toiling with trying to convince their children to not participate in such behaviors, as they tend to lead to self-destruction. Some listen, some do not. Those who do listen, often feel isolated or like they're being left out because they choose not to yield to the negative peer pressures many of their friends are partaking of. Parents have to constantly reassure their children that they're on the right path by not yielding to immorality or self-degradation. I admit that at times, the peer pressures our children are facing can be so intense until, as a parent we too feel this pressure and it will sometimes cause us as parents to second guess whether we're a parent who's too strict or too old fashioned. If you're not careful and don't continue to stand strong as a parent you'll find yourself giving in to what you know is not good for your child. But I say unto those of you who are good parents, don't give in to the pressure! Keep doing what you know is best for your child. Your child may not understand why you won't allow them to do certain things right now, but as they mature, they'll be grateful that you didn't forsake your responsibility as a good parent.

I remember feeling like I was losing my eldest daughter when she started dating and attending college. Whenever I sensed she was battling with something that was against what she'd been taught, I would try to talk to her about it, but it seemed like she couldn't or wasn't hearing me, for the peer pressure that was already in her ears. But I was determined to not give up on her. I kept showing love, support and praying for her. Love draws, hatred repels. God expects us as parents to protect and guide the children He's given us in the way they should go, even if we're not a perfect example of it. If we do this in times of crises with our children, He will either give us new children, like He did for Job or restore the ones we already have, like He did with the Prodigal Son.

Health Crisis

Scripture says Job was also attacked in his health. As if the loss of property, finances and children were not enough, his health was later attacked. Scripture says his body was attacked with painful boils from the sole of his feet to the crown of his head. Job was in pain emotionally, physically, financially and mentally.

Once your health is attacked, it is one of the lowest places to be. When you're sick, with an illness as painful as boils, your entire body is aching. Boils smell and they ooze pus. Being sick will drain your physical strength, energy and take away your appetite. You feel weak. Some people get so bad off, depending on the illness, until they start praying for God to take their life because they're in so much physical pain. Job was definitely in a place to contemplate asking God to take his life. Severe pain in your body has a way of making you want to give up and die, if it's bad enough. In spite of the pain and suffering, Job hung in there. Even though it didn't seem like it, God was with Job. It looked like the end for Job, but it was not. Better days were still in his future. As long as we are alive, there's hope for us to get well. Remain positive. Keep your thoughts up, not down. For negative thoughts form trees with thorns that send out poison to the body. Remember and trust that God can be trusted in your health crisis. No illness is beyond His healing ability. Jesus has already paid for our healing. Healing is one of our constitutional rights in God's Kingdom. So petition for it and claim it.

Relationship Crisis

A major crisis has a way of trying every part of our being and then it moves to try our relationships. Many marriages, family and friendships have been destroyed as a result of a major crisis. In most cases, the crisis causes those in marriages, families, friendships and/or relationships, to turn on each other as a result of prolonged, painful problems that appear unresolvable. I've learned that when a crisis comes, that's the time to bind your forces and support together, not apart. We are stronger together. Job's wife became so miserable until she attacked him with an evil question and suggestion. It was as if she blamed Job for their crisis and so it is with us. We begin to blame one another when things are going wrong for us. Technically though, Job was the cause of their crisis. His fears, unbelief, words and integrity caused their misery.

Out of frustration, Job's wife began to blame him and offer wicked advice. She tried to provoke him to evil. The devil tries this same tactic with us today. When in a relationship crisis, your spouse, family and friends can sometimes say some pretty hurtful things. It can be quite shocking and painful to hear their improper and offen-sive comments. You're already in a very low place and here they come digging you down deeper, instead of lift-ing you higher. But remember this, when your spouse, family members and friends do to you what Job's wife did to him, rebuke them in love and keep your integrity. Always endeavor to keep the peace. When your spouse, family or friends allow the enemy to use them to attack you unjustly, don't take it personally. Forgive them for they know not what they do. After all, crisis is not the time to turn on each other because you need all of your energy for the crisis battle.

If you waste your energy fighting minor matters, when the major battle comes, you won't have enough energy to fight and win. If Job had responded with some unwhole-some words to his wife, he would have done just what Satan wanted and that was, to prove to God that Job wasn't who he appeared to be. It's interesting that even though Job was the one in physical pain, due to the boils, he didn't allow his self to be so weak that he erred in his integrity. He didn't snap on his wife, even though he had plenty of good reasons to do so. His wife went through every crisis he did, except for the boils, yet she reacted like she was the one suffering the most. When in physical pain, we cannot allow our pain to provoke us to becoming belligerent. Job didn't allow his pain to cause him to snap, curse God or die. Besides, what benefit would snapping and cursing have caused? Acting out of character only makes us look bad. It's sign of weakness and carnality. When under extreme pressure and suffering, we must remain Christ-like, level headed and sober. It won't always be easy, but with God it's possible.

Financial Crisis

At the time of my writing this book, unemployment rates are still at an all-time high. Millions of Americans still can't find suitable jobs. At the writing of this book, both my husband and I are not working. In 2009, my husband was laid off after working for a sign company for almost 21 years. In 2010, he obtained another job that was better than the previous one he had.

And then in September 2013, after much waiting, hoping and frustration with there being no opportunities for advancement/promotion, I resigned from an insurance company I'd worked for over seventeen years. I resigned because I felt stuck, held back and unfulfilled. I felt there was "more" for me than what I was experiencing working for this company. I had done all I knew to do in order to move up there such as getting my Bachelor's degree in Organizational Management, a Master's degree in Business Administration, my Professional Academy of Healthcare Management designation, Health and Life insurance license, teaching part-time at a local college and finally, obtaining my real estate license. I had done all of this, while working there full-time, but still no opportunities for advancement came of it. I wasn't getting the return on the investments I'd invested in myself. So after seventeen years, I finally came to the disappointing realization that there were no opportunities for me there, so after much prayer and thought, I resigned believing and trusting God for something greater than what I had experienced. God was using my frustration to provoke me to step out and pursue my destiny. Since all the other things I did, that made sense to do in order to move ahead didn't work, I stepped out in faith, something that didn't make sense. I put in a one week notice and graciously left. Besides, there was no need wasting any more time there. My manager was so angry. He asked me to think about all that the company had done for me. I felt I'd earned everything they'd done for me. I told him I would, but to tell the truth, my mind was already made up, as I had already been thinking about it for over a year. So the next morning, when he came in, the first thing he did was call me at my desk to see whether I had changed my mind. I hadn't. He was furious. The enemy becomes vicious when he sees that we're beginning to move towards our destiny. He raised his voice at me complaining about how I didn't give him a two week notice and how it was peak season in our department. He couldn't believe it. Keep in mind though, that I had warned him nine months earlier that if no opportunities opened up, that I was considering leaving. I visited with him twice about this before finally leaving. I guess he wasn't taking me seriously.

It's interesting how people think they have you figured out or have you on lock down. As a result, they make limiting assumptions about you that are designed to hold you back and control your progress. He saw me as always working there in the same position. I saw myself doing greater things. When those around you have a lower vision for your life than you have, you're with the wrong group. We must surround ourselves with people who are "speaking our language." He began telling me that I would lose my health insurance and my bonus if I quit. Keep in mind that for the previous nine months prior to me doing this, I had been building up my faith like I'd never done before. So nothing he was saying at this point was changing my mind. The "force of faith" had stood up inside me and all I knew was it was time to go! He talked about me to everyone who would listen to him. He made sure I could hear him too. It was if he was trying to provoke me into a confrontation with him. Nevertheless, I stayed professional and kept working to get all my January renewals out before I left. I'm not mad at him, for he knew not what he was doing and didn't understand what I was doing. Like Jacob with Laban in the Bible, I was finally taking charge of my destiny. To him, it didn't make sense, but it made faith to me. Four days later, after my last day there, my husband unexpectedly lost his job. This agitated me at first, but on the other hand I had already expected the enemy to attack my faith in order to cause me to believe I had made the wrong decision. Instead, it actually confirmed that I made the right decision. Otherwise, what's the point of the attack? In the midst of this, I held on to my faith. In hindsight, I now know why I felt the unction and urgency for only a one week notice. If I had given a two week notice, by then my husband would have lost his job and then I probably would have reconsidered resigning. In the end though, God will get the glory! For the enemy had to get His permission to attack my husband. Since God allowed it, I trust He already has victory planned for us. In the meantime, we will continue to walk by faith! I trust we will come out alright, just like we always have.

In the interim, we're going to enjoy the time off together. I admit we're having some enjoyable time together, since we don't have to deal with the hustle and bustle of working right now. We're not stressed. We feel free. In fact, it seem like we're doing better unemployed than we were employed. Resigning my position has given me the opportunity to finally write this book, which I believe is a part of my destiny assignment. It's been absolutely amazing to see the power of God's provision! If we're not walking by faith, we won't see the Supernatural Power of God! During this current economic climate, I've noticed that people are stressed about two things:

1. Because they have a job

2. Because they don't have a job

Every day on the news there's talk about more jobs being cut, more employees being laid off, unemployment benefits being cut, etc. Since I'm a realtor as well, I see more and more people going through bankruptcy, foreclosure and/or the short sale process. We all know that financial crisis in your life at some point is normal, but I've never seen it this bad. Millions of people are struggling.

When Job lost his livestock, he was in a financial crisis, as livestock back then equated to money/wealth. Attacking someone in their finances has the tendency of putting them on edge and sending them into overt hysteria. When people's money is threatened, it's not usual to see them fighting mad, screaming, punching the wall, turning over furniture, going off on people, fussing at their wife, children, cat and dog, etc. No money means, no life. A financial crisis will make you or break you. By the time Satan had finished attacking Job, he didn't have anything left, except his life. But this is all he needed to begin again. As long as we're alive, we have the ability to bounce back from a financial crisis. We just have to calm down and let God show us how to regroup and recover.

I've learned that most of our suffering comes because we're too attached to stuff. We must learn to live our life in a detached manner. That way when financial crises come, we can say what Job said, "Naked came I out of my mother's womb, and naked shall I return thither: the LORD gave, and the LORD hath taken away; blessed be the name of the LORD." When in a financial crisis, we have to learn how to shift gears, such as tightening up our budgets, lowering/eliminating unnecessary expenses, use coupons, buying only sale items, shopping at second hand stores, preparing "left over" meals, etc. We must ask God to help us become more financial savvy and be open to unconventional money management ideas from Heaven, not Babylon. I'm amazed at the financial wisdom/secrets God has taught me. He will teach you how to think differently when it comes to money, if you're open to receive it. Stuff you thought would take years to pay off won't, if you begin to apply God's eccentric financial advice. I'm a witness it works. Because of God's eccentric financial advice, I've been able to pay off a twenty-four month debt in nine months. The only debt I have left to pay off is my house. I'm believing God and working towards paying it off, ahead of schedule. One of the benefits of a financial crisis is it will teach you how to be resourceful, if you're conscious to it. A financial crisis will teach you how to survive and bounce back from the financial crisis. In addition, you'll lose the fear of encountering future financial crises. If you stay focused, keep fighting, and not give up, you will bounce back from your financial crisis. God will cause the financial crisis to work out for your good. Financial crisis prepares us for our next level of financial increase. We go all the way down first and then we go up higher than we were initially. I'm no longer afraid of a financial crisis. I've learned to embrace it and learn the valuable lessons the crisis yields. Financial crises are designed to refine us financially, not destroy us. Financial crises are a sign God has something greater He'd like to get to us, but we must go through the crisis process in order to get it. Don't faint before receiving the good things God has planned for your financial future.

Reputation Crisis

In Scripture, Job's critics/friends accused him of wrong doing, which they believed was the cause of Job's misfortune. So it is today, the critics will always believe the worst about you and your crisis before considering the best about you and your crisis. The critics rarely consider the possibility that you didn't do anything wrong. Job's friend's assumed Job had sinned against God since he was going through so much hell. Incorrect assumptions tend to create rumors that are incorrect and/or damaging, which in turn will ruin a person's reputation. When you're in a crisis, you can expect for people to try to assess you, your crisis and the reason for the crisis. Instead of asking you directly what's going on and whether you're okay, they instead come up with their own story line about your crisis. Instead of praying for you and offering assistance, they criticize you and shun you because they believe the negative rumors. When people say incorrect/derogatory things about you, it's frustrating and embarrassing. You want to confront the gossipers and naysayers. You want to clear up damaging rumors. You almost feel like you should have a press conference in order to clarify incorrect information.

You would think that since the critics were also Job's friends, they'd know better than anybody about Job's character. When you really know a person, you pretty much know what is and is not their character. One thing a crisis will do is show you who's really for you. It will show you what people really think and believe about you.

You know you're in a reputation crisis when people begin to talk down to you, as they no longer respect you or your advice. I remember after we lost our house, I would be in conversation with various family members about matters related to finance/credit and could feel them not receiving my advice/input because of my past foreclosure and bankruptcy. I realized my reputation was no longer perceived as creditable. They responded as if I didn't know what I was talking about.

When people do you like this, God will turn around and raise you up and bless you right in front of your critics. You may temporarily lose your reputation and creditability, but just know that God uses this as free press to highlight how low you were, so that when He blesses you, all your critics will be amazed at how high God took you up. God will take you up so high until your critics will have to pay/bless you just to be in your presence. When God restored Job, his critics brought him gifts. The same people who criticized him had to turn around and bless him. Now that's the kind of restoration we can expect when we come out of a reputation crisis!

Destiny/Purpose Crisis

One of my favorite passages of Scripture is the story of Joseph. Joseph had a great dream, as a result of a great calling on his life. His calling would impact Egypt and surrounding areas. God revealed his purpose via a dream, but He didn't provide the details. I believe this is because God wants us to focus on the dream/promise and not be distracted with the details. It's been said that, "The devil's in the detail." If we knew all the details that precede the fulfilling of our dream, we'd say, "No Thank You, I think I'll pass on that!" Focusing on the details will destroy and paralyze us. If we're not careful, we can sometimes get caught up in over analyzing how our promise is going to come to pass and end up unable to move forward because we become faithless and fearful. This is called, "analysis paralysis." Forget about the details and focus on the promise. We have to keep our eyes on the prize. In the story of Joseph, there are many lessons to glean from it that can serve as "teachable moments" for us, while we're in our crisis, pursuing destiny.

One of the first awful lessons to learn when in a destiny crisis is that sometimes your family will despise you because of your dream/destiny/purpose and at times you'll feel like the Black Sheep of the family. When purpose is on your life, you always tend to feel awkward and out of place when you're around unproductive people and/or an unproductive environment. Your family will try to sabotage you, doubt your gifting, criticize you, throw you in a pit/under the bus and/or sell you out. At times, you may feel fatherless and motherless and sibling less. You will feel abandoned. There will be isolation from family. Joseph went through all of these with his family. Joseph's brothers put him in a pit, sold him as a slave to the Ishmaelites who were on their way to Egypt. When they got to Egypt, Joseph served as a servant/slave in Potiphar's house. In all of this, Scripture says God was with Joseph. Scripture also says that Joseph was successful while working in Potiphar's house, even though how he got there was a setback. When God's hands are on you, no matter how low you go, God will bless you to be successful. Just as He did with Joseph, God will cause everything you do to prosper. You will find favor in the most unlikely places.

When we went through our foreclosure, we found favor with a Spanish woman from South America, who was our landlord. When favor is on your life, it means God has endorsed you. She just so happened to be Christian. Her son David initially met us at her rent house. We explained our foreclosure situation to him. He took a liking to us and told his mom about us. She met us the next day or so at the rent house so she could meet us. When I opened the door of my car, the first statement out of her mouth was, "Oh, you have a Bible in your car!" I always kept my mini Bible in the door pocket of my car so that whenever I'd go to noonday Bible study on Wednesday's, I'd have a Bible to take with me.

To this day, I don't know how she even saw it. She caught me off guard when she pointed out that she saw it because at the time, my mind was on securing a place to live. We found favor in her sight and she rented us her house, when others denied us. At that point, I knew God was with us. I knew things would be alright. God had provision already in place for us every step of the way.

It's no secret that when you're on your journey towards destiny that the enemy will send demons of fear and doubt to speak to you and try to throw you off your path to destiny. But God will be with you at every turn and bump with the provision you need. Setback is a part of success. Failure is a part of success. I've learned that each setback is not a coincidence. Something great is brewing on your behalf!

For a while everything was going well for Joseph and then Potiphar's wife falsely accused Joseph of attempted rape. She, in fact, was the one who wanted to sleep with him, but when he denied her and ran from her, she lied on him and he ended up going to prison.

When we were living in the rent house, there were many days I felt like I was in prison. It was small. I felt so unsettled. We were grateful, but not comfortable. I remember that first Winter there, it was so cold in that house. Since I was not happy to be there, I didn't decorate or anything. There were unpacked boxes in various corners of the house. I thought we wouldn't be there long, but we ended up living there 4 ½ years. According to mortgage loan policy at the time, it takes this long in order to be eligible to apply for another mortgage loan, after going through both foreclosure and bankruptcy back-to-back. When Joseph went to prison, it appeared to be a setback, but actually it was a divine set up. It was a divine connection. I've learned that when we encounter what appears to be a setback, to let go and go with the flow.

Fighting the flow will only delay God's plan and make your situation worse. Sometimes our life will kick into "auto drive" to move us where we need to be. When this happens, we have no control of the steering wheel. Even in prison, God was yet with Joseph. Joseph once again gains favor and mercy. And because He was doing a good job while in prison, the keeper of the prison entrusted the prisoners to him. The keeper of the prison didn't have to watch over Joseph because he knew Joseph had a good work ethic. Whatever Joseph did while in prison, God made it prosper there too. You know you're anointed and gifted when you're favored and prospering even in prison. This is why God doesn't want us to get distracted with the details of our crisis to destiny, because since He's with us, everything will work out in our favor. God is still in control, even when we're down and out. It didn't look like it, but Joseph was on his way up. He was on his way to fulfilling his purpose.

It's important to note that even though Joseph was in Potiphar's house and the prison, places he'd rather not be or deserved to be, he didn't stop utilizing his gift of management and interpreting dreams, even though the dream situation is what got him in this predicament to begin with. Little did he know, but the gift of dreams that got him in this situation, would also get him out of it. Joseph didn't stop living so to speak, just because he was in prison. We don't see where he complained to others about his misfortune or shared what his brothers and Potiphar's wife had done to him. Joseph stayed productive. Scripture says Pharaoh's butler and baker were confined to the king's prison and while there, they each had a dream. Their dreams troubled them, as they didn't know what they meant. They told Joseph about it and he interpreted their dreams. He served them with his gift, when he could have done otherwise. The take away here is, use your gift to help others even though you need help yourself. Don't withhold your gift when you see that it can help somebody. Stir up the gift that's within you! This way when your defining moment comes, you won't be unprepared. Practice makes perfect.

When the butler and baker got out of prison to return serving Pharaoh, Joseph asked them to make mention of him to Pharaoh. This request was a seed of prophetic implication and would come to pass at the appointed time. When the butler got out of prison, he forgot about Joseph, at least temporarily. When you've helped people and then they don't return the favor back, don't fret because God is not going to let your good deeds go without recognition and reward. It's better to let God do for you anyway. And remember, everything that should happen, will happen, when it's time to happen. It was two years later when the butler would make mention of Joseph to Pharaoh, as well as Joseph fulfilling his destiny. Scripture says that one night Pharaoh had a dream. The dream troubled Pharaoh so much until the next morning he called all his advisers/experts together for the interpretation of his dream. None of them were able to interpret his dream. The take away here is, there is an assignment that only you are called to fulfill. There is a problem in this Universe that each of us was born to solve. It's unique to our life experiences, setbacks, crises, pain and suffering.

Since Pharaoh's advisers were not able to interpret his dream, it's at this moment that the butler remembers Joseph. God did not let Joseph be forgotten. The butler told Pharaoh about Joseph and is ability to accurately interpret dreams. Pharaoh summoned Joseph. Joseph not only interprets the dream, but provides a creative solution as well. Joseph then gains favor with Pharaoh.

Pharaoh is so impressed with Joseph's skill and gifting that he promotes Joseph to a top position in his kingdom. Favor took Joseph to the top! One encounter with this type of favor is worth a lifetime of labor! Joseph was finally being compensated for all of his setbacks, crises, pain, suffering, injustices, embarrassments, disappointments, etc. When we make it through our crisis, it's proof that we've become purified gold. And everyone knows gold is expensive and if you want pure gold, you have to pay the price for it. Pharaoh saw Joseph's pure gold and paid Joseph well to have access to it. God is not going to sit back and watch us suffer and not compensate us for our suffering. When Joseph made it to the finish line of his crisis, his value went up dramatically, like stock, and God made sure he was properly compensated. So it shall be with us.

Every time I read this story, it encourages me. Whatever crisis you're in, just know it's not by coincidence. We don't always know the details of our itinerary to purpose, but God has already planned the route we must take to get there. That route may not be the scenic route, the shortest route or the most comfortable route. However, if we will let go and go with the current flow of our life, God will get us to where we're predestined to be. We exist because of purpose. Whether we realize it or not, some of the crisis that occur in our lives are attempting to drive us to our purpose. We all are on the road to purpose. And deep down inside most of us, we know and feel there's something great within us that we've been called to do and need to do. Our job is to yield to the travel arrangements God has already made for us, instead of us trying to make our own travel arrangements. It's so much easier this way even though it appears harder. Crisis is the vehicle through which God uses to drive us to our destiny. And once we arrive at our destiny destination, they'll be a mighty reward and celebration! God restored double to Job, after his crisis. He restored Joseph, after his crisis.

Each paid their dues. Each paid the cost to be boss. God didn't allow any of their pain and suffering to be wasted or go uncompensated. He will do the same for us. Crisis is a character developer. Crisis is the prerequisite to fulfilling destiny. Crisis is God's training ground. Crisis is a catalyst to wealth. Crisis is the innovator of creative ideas and solutions. I believe that as a result of all Joseph's previous crises, they enabled him to provide an economic solution to Pharaoh's dream, which prevented economic crisis in Egypt. Joseph gained all of these as a result of his destiny crisis. If we are successful in coming out of our crisis to purpose, we too will have gain and added value in our lives.

Death Crisis

Death is when something dies. We can experience the death of a marriage, career or with someone dear to us. The death of someone or something is one of the most traumatic experiences we'll ever go through. You will experience all the stages of grief in this type crisis. The crisis of death is devastating because it's the end of a relationship we valued. No more conversations, no more hearing their voice and no more seeing them. Whether expected or unexpected, death is difficult to endure. It's as if the death occurred without our permission. As a result, we feel robbed.

We feel like we can't make it without the person or thing that died. We wonder whether we'll ever smile or be happy again. We find ourselves wondering why the death had to happen. We wonder why God didn't intervene. Job had to be asking these same questions when all of his children died, as it's one thing to lose one child, and an entirely different level of pain to lose all his children at the same time. Even though we ask God why our loved ones had to die, more often than not, we don't receive an answer. We just have to learn how to accept the death and trust that God knows what He is doing. In this life, there will be many things that will happen that we just don't understand. We just have to trust in God's infinite wisdom. His thoughts are not our thoughts and His ways are higher than ours. The take away in this section is, death is a part of living. Only God has control and authority over death. He created us. It's His prerogative to determine who and what will die and when they/it will die.

Besides, no one loves us more than God and if He's allowing a death crisis to incur in our lives, then we must learn to accept what God allows because we are not our own. It may take time, but we can do it. In the meantime, our job is to love, enjoy and make the most of every moment with our loved ones, so we won't have any regrets when the crisis of death comes.

---

CHAPTER 4

12 Steps of Making it Through A Crisis

In order to be successful in accomplishing any goal, one must formulate the steps required to achieve that goal. Completion of each step leads to the completion of the next step and then once all the necessary steps have been completed, the goal will be achieved. The following are twelve steps I've identified as either a result of my past successes and failures or of others I've observed during their crisis.

Step 1– Decide You're Not Going to be Defeated

The first step of working through the crisis is, you must decide that you're not going to be defeated and that you will come through the crisis alright. One of the definitions of crisis is, to decide. You must decide!...decide that you're coming out alright- - not a drug addict, alcoholic, psych patient, sick, a casualty of war or empty handed. Battles are won in our minds first and then on the battle field. Wherever the mind goes, the body will follow. Victory is a choice. You can't be double minded either. Scripture says a double minded man is unstable in all of his ways. We must bring our minds under the influence of triumph!

Step 2 – You Must Build Yourself Up

As with any strenuous and physical event, you must build yourself up spiritually, physically, mentally and emotionally for the upcoming stage of sequence of events. When in a crisis, it can be strenuous and physical. In this step, begin with first determining whether the crisis is demonically motivated or God motivated. This will help you to know which spiritual weapons to use. A demonically motivated crisis is one that is designed to attempt to destroy you because you've been identified as a threat to demonic controlled kingdoms.

A God motivated crisis is designed to develop and prepare you for destiny. It's designed to mature you, stretch and position you for purpose. Both demonic and God motivated crises require spiritual guidance. However, a demonic motivated crisis will require Spiritual, Angelic Military assistance and assault in the spirit realm for breakthrough, which is extremely intense, overwhelming and laborious. Many people do not make it through demonic motivated crises successfully. This type of crisis pulls on every fiber of your being. There's usually some loss in this type of crisis, if you're not trained in spiritual warfare. A God motivated crisis is intense and is won through applying principles and laws. Demonic crises are won via the spirit. God motivated crises are won via the letter - - the Word of God. God motivated crises are designed to develop you and your character in some way. The demonically motivated crisis is designed to develop your spiritual ranking.

So, how do we build ourselves up? In order to build ourselves up, we have to be strategic and selective in what we think, see, hear & speak. We must place ourselves within an environment of victors. We have to get on a consistent schedule of prayer and meditation for intelligence downloads. We have to read uplifting, faith filled materials about triumph. We must listen to motivational music and faith teachings about triumph. We must manage our mouth daily by only making healthy decrees and affirmations, in spite of what we see with our natural eyes. I also like to watch military action movies, as they encourage me and provide strategic revelations about warfare. This might sound crazy, but at certain times we will need talk to ourselves, like a coach would. We must work at doing all of these until we enter what I call, "Rambo Mode." In the movie, "Rambo", there's a point where John Rambo "snaps" so to speak. In this part of the movie, you can see that his eyes are "fixed" in a deep, focused stare as if he's envisioning himself annihilating his enemies. He had entered another realm - - the warfare realm. At this point, he was ready for war. With a stern and focused look in his eyes, he puts on his headband. To me, this prophetically meant he was girding up the loins of his mind, as instructed to do in Scripture. In another part of Scripture, it talks about putting on the whole armor of God so that we'll be able to stand safe against all strategies and tricks of Satan.

This book is providing motivation and strategies to assist you in standing safe during times of personal crisis. It's very critical for us to not enter a crisis without our warfare armor and strategies in place. Some crises require all that I've listed, plus fasting and sometimes giving in some way. Such as giving assistance and encouraging words to someone else while you too are in crisis. It could also mean to give financially as well. I believe the reason some people don't make it successfully through their crisis is because they didn't know how to strategically address their crisis or they under estimated the potency of their crisis. Never under estimate the vigor or intensity of a crisis. We must always have our crisis war chest ready! We must learn to embrace the crisis, if we're going to make it in this life.

Step 3 – Be Patient

In every crisis, be patient and take each day, one at a time. Impatience is an attribute that will destroy us during a crisis, if we don't learn the art of waiting. The spirit of impatience will cause us to feel under pressure and being under pressure can sometimes prevent clarity of mind. It has been said to never make a decision under pressure. This is because we're more likely to make the wrong decision and end up adding more suffering to our crisis. I admit that there are times when a crisis can go on for months and even years. When this happens, we tend to become very impatient because we're extremely tired of waiting for the crisis to end. But I've learned that if you want to come out of your crisis, you <u>must</u> learn to be patient. Scripture says, "Patience is a virtue." Impatience will cause us to attempt to take matters into our own hands, in an attempt to end or resolve the crisis.

When in a prolonged crisis, we will be tempted to resolve the crisis on our own because in our minds, we're speeding things up. In reality, it doesn't speed things up. It makes things worse. We must realize there's an ordained, pre-established and pre-set end date to our crisis and trying to fix/resolve the crisis before that time is a useless and unprofitable effort. We'll come out when it's time to come out, not a second before or after the appointed time. For example, when baking a cake, no matter how hungry you are for the cake, no matter what you do, the cake is not coming out of the oven until it's done. You can watch the oven, pace the floor, keep opening the oven door to check on it, turn the oven temperature up, but this will either cook the cake too fast or burn it up. And then you'll have to start all over again. A good cake takes time. So it is with a crisis. Nothing we do can help bring us out before it's time. So, learn to step back, be patient and take each day one at a time. Let your thoughts think on today only. Think on tomorrow when tomorrow comes; otherwise you'll get over-whelmed and stressed wondering about tomorrow. Wake up each day with an expectancy that today just may be the day you come out of your crisis. And if it turns out you didn't come out that day, be encouraged, knowing it must not be time yet. Apparently all the ar-rangements to your crisis ending date are not complete yet, but be of good cheer, it's near.

Step 4 – Keep Living Your Life

It's no secret that a crisis will consume you, if you let it. So many times when we're in a crisis, if we're not careful, we'll quit living our daily lives and living out our daily routines. We do this because we're emotionally drained, exhausted, depressed, worried, etc., from focusing too much on our crisis. What we focus on the longest becomes strongest in our lives. So if all we think about is our crisis and the problems that come along with it, then the crisis becomes strongest in our lives and we have energy for nothing else. Everything else doesn't matter. Everything else is not important. We don't want to get out of bed or go to work. We don't feel like taking care the kids, going to church, cooking, going to school, hanging out with family and friends, etc. We simply want to be left alone, preferably in a dark room. Sometimes we'll even let our appearance go. We no longer care about how we dress. We'll put on anything almost.

However, I challenge you to do the opposite of all these when you're in a crisis because continuing on with your daily life and routines will help keep you sane. It will prevent you from consistently dwelling on your crisis and keep you from getting stuck. So make plans to hang out with your supportive family and friends. Go to class. Don't let yourself fall behind in school. This would only add to your misery. Besides, the world is not going to stop or slow down, just because you're experiencing a crisis. It keeps moving onward and so must we. If you will continue on with your daily life, you might even get a good laugh in, while at work or while hanging with friends. Lord knows we do need a good laugh during our crisis. As the saying goes, laughter is the best medicine. If need be, go see a good comedy so you can get a good dose of laughter! Dress yourself up like it's fashion week in New York! After all, you are coming out. Don't let the crisis completely stop you from living your life. We must get to the point where when we're in a crisis, no one would even know it, because we're going through with such class and dignity. This is not to make light of your pain or to be pretentious. I'm just saying we must learn to make the best of our crisis, like a mature person and not like a child. Ask yourself, "What can I do to make the best out of where I am right, now?"

Step 5– Don't Make Everyone Else Suffer

Don't make everyone else suffer and/or be miserable just because you're in a crisis. Don't punish innocent by-standers, with a bad attitude. Don't be mean at home, work, school, church, in traffic, etc. Don't take out your frustrations on others. Remember to go through with class and dignity. Just because you're in a crisis, doesn't give you the right or freedom to act rude, cantankerous, combative, confrontational or argumentative with those who have nothing to do with your moment of crisis. Keep your attitude in check. Don't be snappy, quick tempered or unpleasant to be around. This is how a sour loser acts. If you do, however, slip up and behave this way, sincerely apologize and keep it moving. One of your goals is to come through the crisis with the victory, not new enemies or burned bridges, as a result of your shameful behavior. A winner behaves opposite of this because they're confident in their victory and their God!

Step 6 – Watch Out for Mind Tricks

When you're in a crisis, your mind will sometimes play tricks on you. For example, your mind will try to make you believe certain people have it better than you because it appears they never go through a crisis. The truth is, everyone goes through crisis. No one is exempt. It may be they know how to go through their crisis with grace and dignity instead of whining and belly aching about it. In actuality, they may be hurting badly, but choose to keep moving forward believing all will be well. I don't care how much you believe no one else has it as bad as you do, just know there's always someone else dealing with a crisis and sometimes it can be much worse than yours. Everyone has something they're dealing with. We all are trying to make it through our crisis. To you, another person's crisis may seem minor, but to them, it's major and vice versa. Whether we perceive someone else's crisis as minor or major, at the end of the day, it's still a crisis. A crisis we'd rather not endure.

Another trick the mind tries to suggest to you during a crisis is that you're going to lose your mind. You're going to go crazy. You're never going to get out of your crisis. Nobody cares about you. You're a failure. There's no purpose for your life. It's your fault. You did something wrong to deserve the crisis. You should just quit and give up. You're stupid. God doesn't care. It's not meant to be. You're ugly. You're not able/capable. He/she is prettier/handsome than you, smarter than you, thinner than you, got more money than you, they're more outgoing than you. From there, your mind may tell you they're picking on you. They don't like you be cause of your color, because you're educated, not educated, because you're saved/unsaved. And finally, your mind will play tricks on you by telling you, they're putting me down, talking about me. They didn't speak to me. They're jealous of me, intimidated by me, hating on me, they're against me, plotting on me, etc. A crisis can make you flip out, create paranoia and false perceptions. If you see any of these characteristics in yourself or others during a crisis, you'll know that the crisis is now affecting the mental state with false delusions.

Correct it immediately because these thoughts are precursors to suicide and/or homicide. This is a dangerous and vulnerable state of mind to be in. Seek reconciliation with those perceived to be against you. Address your low self-esteem issues. And if people begin telling you that you're acting delusional/bi-polarISH and as if you're about to have a meltdown, don't reject it, receive it. Seriously! Both you and those who are witnessing your abnormal behavior should work towards pursuing you some professional help.

Step 7 – Remember There's an End Date To Your Crisis

Just like in the natural, no storm lasts forever, so it is with a crisis. There is an ending on the way. We sometimes forget this because we feel so overwhelmed and exhausted in our crisis. We feel tired and worn in our body. We wake up day after day with the crisis on our mind. We're dwelling on the crisis, most, if not all day long. Once we've done this for several days, we begin to believe we're not coming out. Our minds start thinking on "What if" scenarios. What if God doesn't deliver me? What if I don't get another job? What if I don't come up with the money? At this point, we have to silence the voice of our mind when it's speaking doubt. Do not tolerate or listen to negative conversations, even the ones in our own mind, for it will talk you into panic and terror, if you let it. Shut it down! Instead, think about how happy you're going to be and how good it's going to feel when the crisis is over. Think on how you'll celebrate coming out of the crisis. Start thanking God in advance for your coming out day! Keep reminding yourself that, "No storm lasts forever."

Step 8 – Remember Past Victories

When we look back over our lives, it's filled with crises God delivered us from that we thought we would not come out of with the victory. It looked like there was no hope. It looked like it was a case too hard for God. It seemed like God wasn't even hearing our prayers regarding the situation. It appeared the tide of the battle was not in our favor. But some kind of way, we overcame the crisis. Some kind of way, things worked out. It's interesting how even though we've been through many crises before, we're always terrified and act like it's our first encounter/rodeo or that it's some strange and new thing happening to us. We must remember that if God brought us out before, he'll do it again and again and again! This is why I believe journaling is a good idea because it's a way to document the crisis (for future review), its circumstances, the pain and the victorious outcome. Over time, you'll be able to go back and see/read how you were in a crisis, how hopeless and agonizing it was and how you made it through it.

Journaling will reduce/remove fear, give you hope, encouragement and cause you to be grateful. As humans, it's sometimes so easy for us to forget the past. When it comes to history, most of us are just not good at remembering it, even though we know history has a way of repeating itself. But during a crisis, we must have total recall of how we overcame previous crises, if we're going to make it through. Journaling will help you to remember past victories. I have several journals. They're a part of my war chest.

Step 9 – Remember Promotion is On the Other Side of the Crisis

In Scripture, there's a story about three Hebrew Boys who were put in the fiery furnace. The furnace was lit seven times hotter than it normally was. As you can imagine, this had to be terrifying. This was definitely a crisis! These Hebrew Boys didn't try to avoid the fiery furnace. They believed that in spite of how bad their situation was, God was going to bring them through it. It's important to note that, even though they believed in God's ability to help them, they still had to go into the fiery furnace. Notice how I keep emphasizing the word "fiery" because this word indicates to us that this was an extraordinary crisis, a major, burning situation. Many times when we're in crisis, it too tends to feel seven times hotter/worse than anything we've gone through. In fact, it feels unbearable. I've learned that sometimes God will allow us to go into the fiery furnace just to show us the magnitude of His power, in ANY situation. We've got to learn that God is well able to deliver us even "in" the fiery furnace. Once we realize and believe this, we won't panic. Seven times hotter doesn't have anything on God's power! If God hasn't showed up the way you thought he should, just go on in the fiery furnace and let God have His perfect work in you.

Scripture says God showed up "in" the fiery furnace "with" the Hebrew Boys and delivered them. When they got out, Scripture says nothing on them was burned. Furthermore, they didn't even smell like smoke, even though the furnace was seven times hotter! Scripture further says that after they came out, they were promoted. Although some crises will be fiery, we must keep in mind that some sort of promotion is on the other side of the crisis. No matter how much it appears the crisis is going to burn us up so to speak, remember—it won't! Don't let the "theatrics" of your crisis intimidate, terrorize or deceive you. God will get in the fire with us and protect us, just like He did with the three Hebrew Boys.

Step 10 – Realize That Crises Are Sent to Develop Us for Future Destiny Purposes

Crises are God's way of developing, refining and maturing us in a specific way in order to prepare, equip and/or train us for our future destiny. For example, when I got married, I was nineteen years old and my husband was twenty-six. My husband was more mature than me, even though back then, I thought I was as mature as he was, but I wasn't.

As with most young people, I was not good with managing money. I hadn't been taught. In fact, when I was in high school, I blew all the pay checks I made. My mother really didn't require that I save. She would fuss about me blowing my money, but never really taught me how to budget. I not only needed to be fussed at, I also needed to be shown "how" to do better with my money. So soon after I was married, I began taking advantage of my husband's credit cards, as he already had established some good credit. As Mrs. Bryson, I began opening accounts and shopping like I didn't have to pay for what I'd charged. My husband would complain about it, but I would keep on shopping and charging.

 Over time, the credit card bills starting building up. The balances were getting higher and higher. Eventually, we fell behind because the payments got out of control. The credit card companies began calling our home every day wanting a payment. The phone calls got so bad, until we would have to leave the phone off the hook until 9:00 at night because they'd stop calling at that time. In all honesty, we were going through a, self-inflicted crisis because of my naïve actions. Nonetheless, not knowing it at first, but God would use this experience to mature me and equip me for my destiny. Even in my ignorance,

God would work it out for my good. One day I was sitting at home worried and stressed about the bills and one of the creditors called. I just so happened to have the phone on the hook that day. She began discussing our account and I began telling her that I didn't know when or how we'd come up with the money to pay the bill. I guess she could hear the agony in my voice because she began to discuss an option of bankruptcy with me. I had never heard of bankruptcy before. She told me that our credit was getting worse each day the account was delinquent and that we should think about filing bankruptcy because it would allow us to get rid of all our debts and start over rebuilding our credit. This information sounded so good to me. I was excited at the possibility of getting free from this bondage. When my husband got home, I told him about it and he thought it was a good idea too, so we scheduled an appointment with a bankruptcy attorney and filed Chapter 13 bankruptcy. We were put on an affordable payment plan and were dis charged from bankruptcy three years later. Once we filed bankruptcy, the phone calls stopped. The burden had been lifted and removed. It was a lesson learned the hard way. The entire situation made me grow up. I learned a valuable lesson about credit cards- - always use cash! I learned about bankruptcy. I didn't know how we'd get out of this mess at the time, but it was worked out for us. We were about to perish, as a result of our lack of knowledge, because we didn't know what to do. But there was help for us. We simply needed the miracle of information. I believe it was God who impressed upon that lady that day to share that bankruptcy information with me that day because I don't know of any creditors who suggests to their clients filing bankruptcy, as doing this is more in my favor than theirs.

After we were discharged from bankruptcy, we didn't owe anyone. Our slate was wiped clean. We were free from financial bondage. Even today, when offered to open a credit card account, I quickly say, "No!" I don't care how much of a discount they're giving for opening a credit card account! Bankruptcy taught me how to live by cash and without credit cards. It's a lesson I'm still practicing today. Three years after being discharged from bankruptcy, we were able to buy our first home. We had a clean credit history and a new home. This was our promotion/reward. It was painful and embarrassing going through this self-inflicted crisis, but with God's help, we came out with new wisdoms related to credit cards. I now use this experience to teach/coach others on money matters.

Step 11 – Don't Yield to Temptation

When you're in a crisis, there will come a time when you'll be tempted to yield to the idea of "self-deliverance." Self-deliverance is when you attempt to deliver yourself by way of taking short cuts or by taking part in self-sabotaging ideas and schemes. Self-deliverance will cause you to get off course to your destiny. This temptation arises out of desperation - - a severe desire for the crisis to be over, by any means necessary. However, we must remember that whatever we compromise on going up the mountain, will control us at the top of the mountain. So don't yield to Satan's temptations. In Scripture, when Jesus was in the wilderness for 40 days and nights, the devil came to Him to try and tempt Him to yield/bow down to him. Jesus was being tempted when He was at his weakest point. And so it will be with us. After enduring the crisis and its effects for such a long period of time, we become tired, stressed, anxious, frustrated, discouraged, weary, etc.

When we're at this point in the crisis, we can expect "temptation thoughts" to plague our mind. At this moment, it seems like yielding to the temptation will provide much needed relief to our agony. In actuality, it yields a false and temporary sense of relief. Yielding will only cause us to mess up what God already has planned for us. Yielding will cause the crisis to become worse.

Yielding will also cause us to have to repeat the crisis because we "cheated" so to speak and failed to come out with victory, God's way. I've learned that whatever our temptation thoughts may be, the reward God has for us, if we don't yield, is far greater than what we're being tempted to yield/bow down to. If we don't yield, but go on through the crisis, we'll be so happy we did! Just think how badly things could have turned out if Jesus had yielded to the devil.

Every temptation the devil presented, Jesus rejected it. The devil tried to be devious by quoting manipulative Scriptures, in order to trick Jesus into yielding/bowing down to him. In other words, the devil tried to use strategic justification via Scripture to convince Jesus to yield. If we're not careful, the devil's reasons for yielding/bowing down will almost sound rational. It will sound like the provision we need. It will sound like it's what will resolve our crisis. Satan will try to offer us what we already have or are. He asked Jesus to turn the stone into bread, when Jesus is the bread of life. We can't be so weary and desperate that we miss our blessing all because we came under the influence of the devil's lies, like a drunken person. When we're under the influence of anything, it's intoxicating and controlling. Satan used this same tactic on Eve. So be sober and alert because he will try this same strategy on us, when we're our weakest. We can't allow ourselves to yield to the devil's solution to our crisis, we must decide to keep trusting and waiting on God, to the end. No matter how good the devil's idea sounds, God is our only trusted help.

After the birth of our eldest daughter in 1993, my husband and I knew we'd one day try for another child. In 1998 I became pregnant again. It was a boy. However, at the start of my second trimester, I miscarried. Little did I know that I would continue to miscarry for the next fourteen years. But with each pregnancy and loss, my husband and I kept believing God for a second child. But the miscarriages kept happening and the doctor and hospital bills kept incurring. I became depressed. We incurred emotional scarring. We incurred embarrassment, as people were wondering why we would continue trying when we had already had several losses and had gone through so much disappointment and pain, but I was like Dr. Martin Luther King Jr., I had a dream!...a dream of having more than one child!

At one point, I remember being in competition with the losses. It was like I had in my mind that I would not let this miscarriage thing beat me. It was like I had a secret rivalry going on with my miscarriages, as I desperately wanted to prove I could beat this. The doctors weren't able to tell me why I kept having this problem. Family and friends began to suggest that my husband and I adopt a child. I know they meant well, but I didn't want a child via adoption. This was temptation talk to me. I remember telling them that I wanted a child that was created intimately with my husband's sperm and my egg. I don't have anything against adoption and I wasn't trying to be rude, just unwavering in my faith on this. Besides, to me adopting a child was yielding to unbelief. Plus, even though I kept having miscarriages, afterwards I would have a dream of me nursing my baby. I couldn't tell whether it was a boy or girl, even though I wanted a son this time. I was only able to see that I did have a baby and I was breastfeeding it.

Looking back, I now realize it was God letting me know that despite all of the other miscarriages, I would birth a second child. For this reason, I would not yield to the temptation thoughts or suggestions. However, over time, I decided not to try so hard in having a second child. I decided to stop trying to make it happen, but let it happen. I surrendered it to God. When I did this, the burden and tussling of it all left my body and a hefty dose of peace came all over me. I let it go. I let it go to the point that it didn't even matter anymore whether I had a second child or not. This is when I got pregnant and successfully brought forth our second child. She was born during a revival in 2007. I went to revival that Friday night, helped pray for some people and on that Saturday morning, my water broke. Fourteen years later we birthed another beautiful daughter. The pregnancy was great and was without any problems or complications. No bed rest had to be prescribed, this time. No spotting, this time. No vomiting, this time. My pregnancy was amazing! I was in God's timing. I was moving in God's appointed time for our second child. His timing included pregnancy bliss! Nothing could touch me or harm me or cause another miscarriage, THIS TIME!!

Now just think if I had yielded to the temptation suggestion to adopt. It would have been an Ishmael/Isaac situation- - my plot vs. God's perfect will. I'm so glad we waited on God! Every time I look at Miracle, I get encouraged because she is a living, constant reminder that God keeps His promises and that He is able to do any thing.   Miracles still do happen! I'm a witness! And now I'm able to share this story with others, encouraging and coaching them to not yield to temptation thoughts and to not settle for anything less than your promise. Doing so will set you back. Yielding says, "I'm not going to wait on God to deliver me." It says," I'm taking matters into my own hands." Not yielding says, "I'm tired, hurting and desperate, but I choose to wait on God to get me through this." Each choice has a reward. It's up to us which reward we'll receive. I can tell you from experience, waiting on God is worth the wait!

Step 12 – The Silence is Normal

One of the hardest moments to endure during a crisis is the silence. When I say silence, I mean the moments when it seems God is not speaking back to you, in spite of your constant praying to Him. It's also a type of silence where it seems no one is even thinking about you. No phone calls, emails, text messages and no packages

through U.S. Mail. When in a crisis, your main objective
is to find a solution to your crisis. During this period of
silence, you're praying and anticipating that your an-
swer/solution is coming possibly via a phone call, email,
text message or U.S. Mail. In fact, you're checking each
of these avenues daily for your answer/solution. You're
hoping each day you wake up will be the day of deliverance from the crisis only to get to the close of another
day with silence. At this point, you're asking yourself
whether anybody is thinking about you. Did the em-
ployers get your resume? Will they call you for an inter-
view? Will the bank approve your home loan? Will the
bank approve your modification request? Where will
you get the money to avoid foreclosure? Will someone
unexpectedly bless you with some money? How will this
crisis be resolved since you don't see how?

These are examples of the various questions running
through people's minds in this country, during this crisis
season. At this point, you're just barely believing God for

divine assistance. You're holding on by a wing and a prayer. You're wondering why God seems to be so silent. Doesn't He care? It has been said that the teacher doesn't talk during the test. When God is silent, it's because we're being tested. God wants to see how well we can navigate through the crisis. After all, He has chosen us, for such a time as this. He wants to see what He put into us come out of us.

Obstacles are God's goldsmith that brings forth the pure gold God placed inside us. We don't know the full extent of what God has placed inside of us, but God does. This is why He's never nervous about our inability to overcome the crisis, as ability is within us. He designed us to withstand and overcome every earthly crisis. His DNA is within us. Therefore, we are more than able to triumph over trouble! In fact, we're not in trouble, we're in transition! We're about to shift! When we're in this phase of the crisis, I suggest that you begin praising and worshipping God and watch your breakthrough break forth. As you go up in praise and worship, you can go up so high, so to speak, until something will snap in your spirit. And a feeling of peace will come over you affirming everything is alright.

Several years ago, my husband and I had bought our second home. It was our dream home. We felt God blessed us with it too. With all the hurt from the miscarriages and since it seemed the second baby hadn't come yet, we began to focus on moving into our dream home. We went all in on this dream. We sacrificed everything.

In looking back though, we were compensating for the miscarriages. I know now, there's a danger in doing this. At any rate, a year or so after living in the house, we encountered a financial crisis as a result of our teenaged daughter running up our cell phone bill into the thousands. This was such an unexpected blow, especially since we were running a tight budget. Our mortgage payment was hefty to say the least. Like most people, when an unexpected expense comes, we had to juggle our other bills in order to try to pay off our cell phone bill, before they turned off our phones. To make matters worse, our second car broke down. This was another unexpected expense. Since we lived outside the city limits, it was imperative that we have two means of transportation, so we got our car fixed. Sometimes no matter how well we budget our income, the bottom line is, we need more money!

By this time, we're robbing Peter to pay Paul and then borrowing again from Peter. It was horrible. As you probably have already guessed, it became very difficult to get caught back up on our bills, especially since we were already running a tight budget. We began to fall behind on our mortgage payments. If you know anything about foreclosure, you know it usually takes about three months before the bank will begin to threaten foreclosure. This is where we were. All I could say at this point was, "Oh, God!" We didn't know what to do, as we'd never gone through foreclosure before. I did know, however, that I didn't want to lose my dream home. After all, this would be humiliating, especially since we believed and told everyone that God blessed us with our dream home. I began to pray and call on God…aggressively! I prayed, prayed and prayed some more. I kept going to church and work as if nothing was wrong. Then one day, we got a letter with a scheduled foreclosure date.

As I was reading the letter, I felt my spirit drop. The only thing I knew to do was pray to God and keep believing God. This is just how much I believed in His ability to help us. We needed a divine intervention. In the meantime, I submitted a request for a loan modification with our mortgage company, as the letter stated we could do. We mailed off the paperwork to the mortgage company. We were anxious to hear their response, but our contact at the mortgage company was not very responsive. We needed to know whether we'd been approved. Now comes the temptation thoughts of: "Go see a bankruptcy attorney to see if you can file bankruptcy and keep your house." Since the country was in a recession, bankruptcy commercials geared towards foreclosure were numerous and recurrent. So at the time, it seemed the logical thing to do was to visit with a bankruptcy attorney. I made an appointment, but God provided a way of escape. I say this because the payment plan the attorney came up with was way more than we were already paying. There was no way I was going to agree to this alternative. Since this option didn't work out for us, I knew then that God would have to be the one to deliver us. Besides, we didn't know it at the time, but we'd need to save this option for later. I was all out of solutions, but I was not out of prayer and faith. We didn't have the money we needed, so I used what I had - - prayer and my faith.

As an act of faith that we would not lose our home, we went to Home Depot to get some mulch to refresh our landscaping. This was definitely an act of faith because who does this when they know they're on the verge of foreclosure? After all this would be a waste of money, right? Well we did! Faith without works is dead. More days went by, drawing us closer to the scheduled foreclosure date. We still hadn't received a response from the mortgage company. However, we're still standing in faith and the pressure is on. In the meantime, I wanted a second telephone line in our house for a fax machine, as I was in the process of trying to get our home office set up for an upcoming project I was working on.

So one day I had to meet the telephone technician at the house so he could install the line. I thought about cancelling it, but decided not to as an act of my faith. We were still praying and believing God that we wouldn't lose our home. At any rate, I left work on my lunch break to meet the technician. On the drive home, as you can imagine, the foreclosure issue was heavily on my mind. In an attempt to get some relief, I turned on my CD player in the car. I began praising and worshipping God. I was using what I had. The praise and worship got stronger and stronger. I was praising God, worshipping God and talking to God. Tears were flowing and then I felt what I can only describe as a "snap" within me and then a strong peace or as some say, blessed assurance came over me. It made me feel/know that everything was alright. I was calm inside. When I arrive at the house, I didn't park in the garage like I normally did, since I had to return back to work. I entered the house through the front door.

When I got to the front door, I noticed a FedEx package. It was from the mortgage company. I went inside the house and opened it and read it. The letter said our modification had been approved! It listed our new, slightly higher payment amount, as well as the amount of money we needed in order to reinstate the loan. You talk about happy and rejoicing! I was so very, very, very joyful! I didn't know what to do with myself. I was trembling, because I'd seen the glory of God, again, but in a new and different way! God saved us! God delivered us! Even though there had been silence for a while, it was because God was working things out behind the scene. When our crisis situation is quiet the most and it appears nothing or no one is moving on our behalf, that's when God is moving for us the most. All God need for us to do is, use what we have and then navigate through the crisis via the principles of Scripture that we've been taught over the years, as a result of walking with Him and serving Him.

If we work the Word of God, it will work for us! When you're in the silence phase of your crisis, don't be deceived by the silence, just remember, THE SILENCE IS NORMAL!

Conclusion

Several years ago, I was prophesied to that I would write a book. After years of going through "the process," the pieces finally came together for me to fulfill that prophecy. I did not know, however, that I would have to go through so much pain and misery in order to birth this book. My misery caused me to write this book, as I believe the information in it will help others overcome life and its various crises.

It's a blessing and an opportunity for me to have come through my crises and share the wisdom gained from some of them, especially since I'm usually a private person. But God has called me forth to make my story public so I could tell you that: In every crisis, we are not alone. God is with us. We're not in trouble, we're in transition. We are not without help and resources. God provides the provisions we need. No crisis is too great that we can't overcome it and be restored. Each crisis has a take away God wants us to get. Crises reveal our inner strengths that we don't know we possess. Crises have a way of cutting soul ties in our life so we can make decisions we've been avoiding. Crisis is God's way of trying to give us experience so we'll have the authority in an area. There may be losses during our crises, but we mustn't lose God or lose ourselves. We can't let fear stop us from trusting in God's ability to help us, no matter how afraid we are while in our crisis. We must always hold on to our faith while in a crisis. Don't forget that fear and no faith create crises, so it's imperative that we live each day fearless and in faith. While in the crisis, don't be deceived by the deceptions that you're not coming out or that there's no hope for you. Remember, prayer is the doorway to the Spirit of answers, when we don't know what to do. With God, we are well able to come out of any crisis with the victory! For no weapon formed against us shall prosper! To God be the Glory!

ABOUT THE AUTHOR

Keeler Bryson is a Teacher, Motivational Speaker, Life Coach and Author. She holds a Bachelor's of Arts degree in Organizational Management, a Master's degree in Business Administration and a Ph.D. in Overcoming a Hard-Knock-Life. She is the founder of Teachable Life Moments, LLC and Vision Writers Publishing, LLC.

She is the author of the book, <u>Crisis Management: How To Manage Personal Life Crises</u> a book she was inspired to write as a result of repeated, overwhelming, devastation in her life. In the book she coaches the reader through the process of personal life crises by sharing personal crises she's experienced and the principles that helped her emerge from them successfully. After becoming an experienced crisis overcomer, Keeler now lives with a passion to encourage, equip and inspire others to be overcomers so that they can fulfill their purpose.

She's happily married to Grover Bryson for over 20 years.
They have two daughters, Whitney and Miracle.

I Want To Hear From You!

If this book has inspired or helped you in any way, write me or email me and share your story.

Teachable Life Moments, LLC

P.O. Box 6516

Sherwood, AR 72124

Email: Keeler@KeelerBryson.com

Website: www.KeelerBryson.com

Twitter: @KeelerSavant

Need Coaching?

Throughout my life I've experienced several experiences that have caused me to become purposely exceptional.

Therefore, I've made my knowledge and life experiences available to share and/or coach others successfully through their personal life crises.

If you would like experienced, quality and effective coaching, please feel free to contact me at, Coaching@KeelerBryson.com or visit www.KeelerBryson.com for more information.

Inspired,

Keeler Bryson

www.ingramcontent.com/pcd-product-compliance
Lightning Source LLC
LaVergne TN
LVHW021522080426
835509LV00018B/2614